JUST KIDDING!

Silly Stories

By Paul Virr

Illustrated by Amanda Enright
and Kasia Dudziuk

WINDMILL
BOOKS ™

Published in 2020 by Windmill Books,
an Imprint of Rosen Publishing
29 East 21st Street, New York, NY 10010

Cataloging-in-Publication Data

Names: Virr, Paul.
Title: Silly stories / Paul Virr.
Description: New York : Windmill Books, 2020. | Series: Just kidding! | Includes glossary
and index.
Identifiers: ISBN 9781538391280 (pbk.) | ISBN 9781538391303 (library bound) |
ISBN 9781538391297 (6 pack)
Subjects: LCSH: Wit and humor, Juvenile. | Riddles, Juvenile.
Classification: LCC PN6166.V577 2019 | DDC 818'.602 --dc23

Manufactured in the United States of America

CPSIA Compliance Information: Batch BS19WM: For Further Information contact Rosen Publishing, New York, New York at 1-800-237-9932

Contents

Fairy-Tale Fun!................................4

Jokes Ahoy!................................6

Wacky Woodland!................................8

Jumbo Jokes................................12

Playful Penguins................................14

Ridiculous Robots! 18

Un-bear-ably Funny!................................20

Fairyland Funnies!................................22

Space Sillies!................................24

Hopping Around!................................28

What's the Buzz?................................30

Glossary, Index................................32

Fairy-Tale Fun!

Why do dragons sleep during the day?
So they can fight knights!

Why is a fairy-tale king like a piece of wood?
Because he's a ruler!

5

Jokes Ahoy!

Why couldn't the pirates play cards?
Because their captain was standing on the deck!

What do you call a pirate without an eye patch or a wooden leg?
A beginner!

Wacky Woodland!

Jumbo Jokes

Which game should
you never play with an
elephant?
Squash!

Why are elephants
so wrinkly?

Have you ever tried
to iron an elephant?

What do you get if you cross elephants with fish?
Swimming trunks!

What do you call the king of the giraffes?
Your high-ness!

Playful Penguins

Ridiculous Robots!

What do you call a robot that loves swimming?
Rusty!

How can you get a robot to come to your birthday party?
Send it a tin-vitation!

19

Un-bear-ably Funny!

What do you call bears with no ears?

Bees!

What kind of gym shoes do bears wear?

They don't wear any. They go bear-foot!

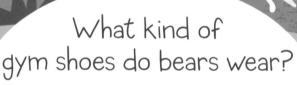

Fairyland Funnies!

Space Sillies!

Hopping Around

How did the frog feel when it hurt its foot? **Un-hoppy!**

What fast food do frogs like best? **French flies!**

What's the Buzz?

What are the cleverest insects?
Spelling bees!

How do bees get to school?
They catch the school buzz!

Why do bees have sticky hair?

They use honeycombs!

What flies through the air and goes "zzub, zzub"?

A bee flying backward!

Glossary

black hole An invisible area in outer space that light cannot get out of.

deck A platform of a ship, or a pack of playing cards.

heavy metal A style of music that is loud with a hard beat.

hip-hop A rhythmic style of music that is often accompanied by rhyming speech.

honeycomb Hexagonal cells built by honeybees to keep their young and store honey.

iceberg A large, floating mass of ice.

Index

A
aliens 24–27

B
bears 20–21
bees 20, 30–31
birthday 18
black hole 25
bunnies 8, 10

C
cards 6
Cinderella 5

D
dragons 4, 5

E
elephants 12, 13

F
fairies 22–23
fairy tales 4–5
frogs 28–29

G
gardener 24
giraffe 13
gym 20

I
icebergs 16
invitation 18

K
knights 4, 5

M
music 10, 19

P
penguins 14–17
pirates 6–7

R
robots 18–19
rocket 26

S
school 5, 22, 30
soccer 5
squirrels 9, 11

W
woodland 8–11